THE NEW NATION
1789–1850

STUDENT STUDY GUIDE

OXFORD

UNIVERSITY PRESS

Oxford University Press, Inc., publishes works that
further Oxford University's objective of excellence
in research, scholarship, and education.

Oxford   New York
Auckland   Cape Town   Dar es Salaam   Hong Kong   Karachi
Kuala Lumpur   Madrid   Melbourne   Mexico City   Nairobi
New Delhi   Shanghai   Taipei   Toronto

With offices in
Argentina   Austria   Brazil   Chile   Czech Republic   France   Greece
Guatemala   Hungary   Italy   Japan   Poland   Portugal   Singapore
South Korea   Switzerland   Thailand   Turkey   Ukraine   Vietnam

Published by Oxford University Press, Inc.
198 Madison Avenue, New York, NY 10016
www.oup.com

ISBN 978-0-19-522319-4 (California edition)   ISBN 978-0-19-518883-7

Writer: Kent Krause
Project Manager: Matt Fisher
Project Director: Jacqueline A. Ball
Education Consultant: Diane L. Brooks, Ed.D.
Design: designlabnyc

Casper Grathwohl, Publisher

Printed in the United States of America
on acid-free paper

Dear Parents, Guardians, and Students:

This study guide has been created to increase student enjoyment and understanding of *The New Nation*.

The study guide offers a wide variety of interactive exercises to support every chapter. At the back of the guide are activity maps to help tie your study of history to the study of geography. Also, you will find several copies of a library/media center research log to use to organize your time researching proejcts and assignments. Parents or other family members can participate in activities marked "With a Parent or Partner." Adults can help in other ways, too. One important way is to encourage students to create and use a history journal as they work through the exercises in the guide. The journal can simply be an off-the-shelf notebook or three-ring binder used only for this purpose. Some students might like to customize their journals with markers, colored paper, drawings, or computer graphics. No matter what it looks like, a journal is a student's very own place to organize thoughts, practice writing, and make notes on important information. It will serve as a personal report of ongoing progress that your child's teacher can evaluate regularly. When completed, it will be a source of satisfaction and accomplishment for your child.

Sincerely,

Casper Grathwohl
Publisher

This book belongs to:

_____

CONTENTS

HOW TO USE THE
STUDENT STUDY GUIDES TO
A HISTORY OF US

One word describes A History of US: stories. Every book in this series is packed with stories about people who built a brand new country like none before. You will meet presidents and politicians, artists and inventors, ordinary people who did amazing things and had wonderful adventures. The best part is that all the stories are true. All the people are real.

As you read this book, you can enjoy the stories while you build valuable thinking and writing skills. The book will help you pass important tests. The sample pages below show special features in all the History of US books. Take a look!

Before you read

- Have a notebook or extra paper and a pen handy to make a history journal. A dictionary and thesaurus will help you too.

- Read the chapter title and predict what you will learn from the chapter. Note that often the author often adds humor to her titles with plays on words or **puns**, as in this title.

- Study all maps, photos, and their captions closely. The captions often contain important information you won't find in the text.

27 Howe Billy Wished France Wouldn't Join In

General Howe had already served in America. In 1759 he led Wolfe's troops to seize Quebec.

A **hoop-stay** was part of the stiffening in a skirt; a **japon** was part of a corset. **Matrons** are married women. The **misses** are single girls; **swains** and **beaux** are young men or boyfriends. **Making love** meant flirting. **British Grenadiers** are part of the royal household's infantry.

Sir William Howe (who was sometimes called Billy Howe) was in charge of all the British forces in America. It was Howe who drove the American army from Long Island to Manhattan. Then he chased it across another river to New Jersey. And, after that, he forced George Washington to flee on—to Pennsylvania. It looked as if it was all over for the rebels. In New Jersey, some 3,000 Americans took an oath of allegiance to the king. But Washington got lucky again. The Europeans didn't like to fight in cold weather.

Sir William settled in New York City for the winter season. Howe thought Washington and his army were done for and could be

Swarming with Beaux

Rebecca Franks was the daughter of a wealthy Philadelphia merchant. Her father was the king's agent in Pennsylvania, and the family were Loyalists. Rebecca visited New York when it was occupied by the British. Her main interest in the war was that it meant New York was full of handsome officers:

My Dear Abby, By the by, few New York ladies know how to entertain company in their own houses unless they introduce the card tables....I don't know a woman or girl that can chat above half an hour, and that on the form of a cap, the colour of a ribbon or the set of a hoop-stay or jupon....Here, you enter a room with a formal set curtsey and after the how do's, 'tis a fine, or a bad day, and those trifling nothings are finish'd, all's a dead calm till the cards are introduced, when you see pleasure dancing in the eyes of all the matrons....The misses, if they have a favorite swain, frequently decline playing for the pleasure of making love....Yesterday the Grenadiers had a race at the Flatlands, and in the afternoon this house swarm'd with beaux and some very smart ones. How the girls wou'd have envy'd me cou'd they have peep'd and seen how I was surrounded.

126

6

As you read

- Keep a list of questions.

- Note the bold-faced definitions in the margins. They tell you the meanings of important words and terms – ones you may not know.

- Look up other unfamiliar words in a dictionary.

- Note other sidebars or special features. They contain additional information for your enjoyment and to build your understanding. Often sidebars and features contain quotations from primary source documents such as a diary or letter, like this one. Sometimes the primary source item is a cartoon or picture.

finished off in springtime. Besides, Billy Howe loved partying. And some people say he liked the Americans and didn't approve of George III's politics. For reasons that no one is quite sure of, General Howe just took it easy.

But George Washington was no quitter. On Christmas Eve of 1776, in bitter cold, Washington got the Massachusetts fishermen to ferry his men across the Delaware River from Pennsylvania back to New Jersey. The river was clogged with huge chunks of ice. You had to be crazy, or coolly courageous, to go out into that dangerous water. The Hessians, on the other side—at Trenton, New Jersey—were so sure Washington wouldn't cross in such bad weather that they didn't patrol the river. Washington took them by complete surprise.

A week later, Washington left a few men to tend his campfires and fool the enemy. He quietly marched his army to Prince-ton, New Jersey, where he surprised and beat a British force. People in New Jersey forgot the oaths they had sworn to the king. They were Patriots again.

Those weren't big victories that Washington had won, but they certainly helped American morale. And American morale needed help. It still didn't seem as if the colonies had a chance. After all, Great Britain had the most feared army in the world. It was amazing that a group of small colonies would even attempt to fight the powerful British empire. When a large English army (9,500 men and 138 cannons) headed south from Canada in June 1777, many observers thought the rebellion would soon be over.

The army was led by one of Britain's

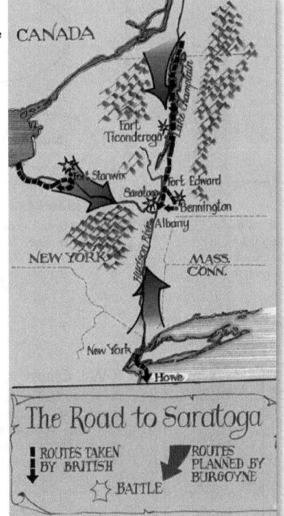

The Road to Saratoga

ROUTES TAKEN BY BRITISH

ROUTES PLANNED BY BURGOYNE

BATTLE

General Burgoyne's redcoats carried far too much equipment. Each man's boots alone weighed 12 pounds. They took two months to cover 40 miles from Fort Ticonderoga to Saratoga, and lost hundreds of men to American snipers.

127

After you read

- Compare what you have learned with what you thought you would learn before you began the chapter.

The next two pages have models of graphic organizers. You will need these to do the activities for each chapter on the pages after that. Go back to the book as often as you need to.

GRAPHIC ORGANIZERS

As you read and study history, geography, and the social sciences, you'll start to collect a lot of information. Using a graphic organizer is one way to make information clearer and easier to understand. You can choose from different types of organizers, depending on the information.

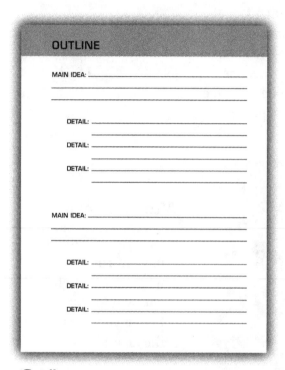

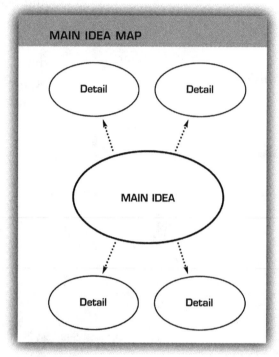

Outline

To build an outline, first identify your main idea. Write this at the top. Then, in the lines below, list the details that support the main idea. Keep adding main ideas and details as you need to.

Main Idea Map

Write down your main idea in the central circle. Write details in the connecting circles.

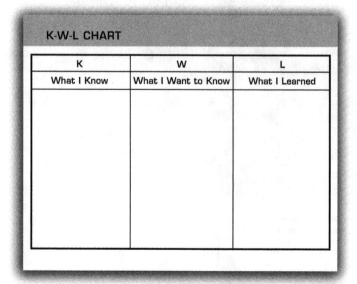

K-W-L Chart

Before you read a chapter, write down what you already know about a subject in the left column. Then write what you want to know in the center column. Then write what you learned in the last column. You can make a two-column version of this. Write what you know in the left and what you learned after reading the chapter.

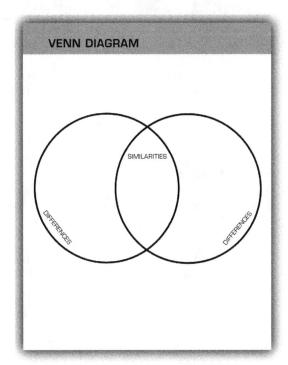

Venn Diagram

These overlapping circles show differences and similarities among topics. Each topic is shown as a circle. Any details the topics have in common go in the areas where those circles overlap. List the differences where the circles do not overlap.

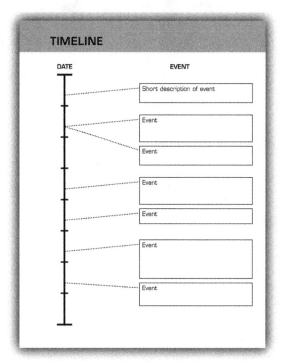

Timeline

A timeline divides a time period into equal chunks of time. Then it shows when events happened during that time. Decide how to divide up the timeline. Then write events in the boxes to the right when they happened. Connect them to the date line.

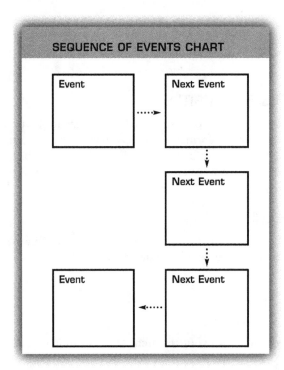

Sequence of Events Chart

Historical events bring about changes. These result in other events and changes. A sequence of events chart uses linked boxes to show how one event leads to another, and then another.

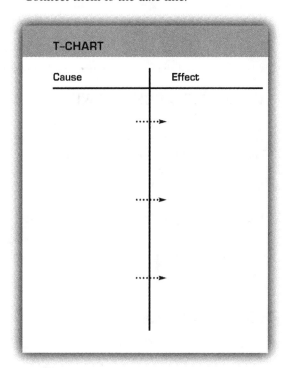

T–Chart

Use this chart to separate information into two columns. To separate causes and effects, list events, or causes, in one column. In the other column, list the change, or effect, each event brought about.

REPORTS AND SPECIAL PROJECTS

Aside from the activities in this Study Guide, your teacher may ask you to do some extra research or reading about American history on your own. Or, you might become interested in a particular story you read in *A History of US* and want to find out more. Do you know where to start?

GETTING STARTED

The back of every *History of US* book has a section called "More Books to Read." Some of these books are fiction and some are nonfiction. This list is different for each book in the series. When you want to find out more about a particular topic from the reading, these books are a great place to start—and you should be able to find all of them in your school library.

Also, if you're specifically looking for *primary sources*, you can start with the *History of US Sourcebook and Index*. This book is full of *primary sources*, words and evidence about history directly from the people who were involved. This is an excellent place to find the exact words from important speeches and documents.

DOING RESEARCH

For some of the group projects and assignments in this course, you will need to conduct research either in a library or online. When your teacher asks you to research a topic, remember the following tips:

TO FIND GOOD EVIDENCE, START WITH GOOD SOURCES

Usually, your teacher will expect you to support your research with *primary sources*. Remember that a primary source for an event comes from someone who was there when the event took place. The best evidence for projects and writing assignments always comes from *primary sources,* so if you can't seem to find any right away, keep looking.

ASK THE LIBRARIAN

Librarians are amazing people who can help you find just about anything in the library. If you can't seem to find what you're looking for, remember to ask a librarian for help.

WHEN RESEARCHING ONLINE, STICK TO CREDIBLE WEBSITES

It can be difficult to decide which websites are credible and which are not. To be safe, stick with websites that both you and your teacher trust. There are plenty of online sources that have information you can trust to be correct, and usually they're names you already know. For example, you can trust the facts you get from places like pbs.org, census.gov, historychannel.com, and historyofus.com. In addition to free websites like these, check with your librarian to see which *databases and subscription-based websites* your school can access.

USE THE LIBRARY/MEDIA CENTER RESEARCH LOG

At the back of this study guide, you'll find several copies of a Library/Media Center Research Log. Take one with you to the library or media center, and keep track of your sources. Also, take time to decide how helpful and relevant those sources are.

OTHER RESOURCES

Your school and public library have lots of additional resources to help you with your research. These include videos, DVDs, software, and CDs.

CHAPTER 1

THE FATHER OF OUR COUNTRY

SUMMARY *George Washington was elected the first president of the United States. Crowds cheered Washington as he rode to New York to take office.*

ACCESS

Imagine that you could interview George Washington after his inauguration. In your history journal make a list of five questions you would ask the new president. One question might be "How do you feel about being the first president?" Read the chapter carefully and write the answers to the questions as you imagine Washington might answer them.

WORD BANK

tsars   monarchy   armory   inauguration   president-elect

Choose words from the word bank to complete the sentences. One word is not used at all.

1. A government that is run by a king or queen is called a _____.

2. The _____ is the person who has been elected president but has not yet taken office.

3. Kings and queens ruled Spain, and _____ ruled Russia.

4. On April 30, 1789, George Washington took the oath as president at his _____.

WORD PLAY

In the dictionary, look up the word you did not use. Write a sentence using that word.
Write a sentence that includes two of the words in the word bank.

_____

_____

WORKING WITH PRIMARY SOURCES

Abigail Adams wrote these words to describe George Washington:

> He is polite with dignity, affable without familiarity, distant without haughtiness, grave without austerity, modest, wise, and good.

Note the seven qualities that Adams lists. On your own or as part of a small group, think about how these qualities would help a person be a good president. Then think of examples from George Washington's life that demonstrate the traits listed. Write your thoughts in your history journal, or help your group prepare a report that could be delivered to the rest of the class.

WRITING

Washington was gracious as the crowds cheered him. To be gracious means to be

proud   excited   humble   angry

Circle your answer. In your history journal, write about a time when you were gracious.

ABOUT BEING A PRESIDENT

SUMMARY *George Washington chose advisers to help him run the country.*

ACCESS

Have you ever tried to do a really hard job by yourself? Hard jobs are usually easier when you get people to help. President Washington could not run the country by himself. He needed advisers to assist him. Copy the main idea map from page 8 into your history journal. In the largest circle, put Washington's name. In each of the smaller circles, write the name of one of the people who helped Washington govern the nation. Below each name, write the job that the person had.

WORD BANK   precedent   executive   legislative   judicial   cabinet   dictatorship

Choose words from the word bank to complete the sentences. One word is not used at all.

1. The _____ branch includes the nation's courts.

2. A government that is run by an all-powerful leader is called a _____.

3. The president is the head of the _____ branch.

4. Washington chose Henry Knox to serve in his _____.

5. Congress is also called the _____ branch.

WORD PLAY

In the dictionary, look up the word you did not use. Write a sentence using that word.

_____

WITH A PARENT OR PARTNER

The United States has a three-branch government. Write the name of each branch at the top of a piece of paper. Below each name, write five words that relate to that particular branch of government. Ask a parent or partner to do the same. Then read your lists to each other.

WORKING WITH PRIMARY SOURCES

In 1792 Dr. Benjamin Rush wrote this about a hot air balloon flight by Jean-Pierre François Blanchard:

> For some time days past the conversation in our city has turned wholly upon Mr. Blanchard's late Aerial Voyage. It was truly a sublime sight. Every faculty of the mind was seized, expanded and captivated by it, 40,000 people concentrating their eyes and thoughts at the same instant, upon the same object, and all deriving nearly the same degree of pleasure from it.

1. How did Benjamin Rush feel about Blanchard's flight?

2. How did the people of Philadelphia feel about Blanchard's flight?

WRITING

Imagine that you are in Philadelphia watching Blanchard's flight. In your history journal, write a letter to a friend describing the event in your own words.

CHAPTER 3

THE PARTIES BEGIN

SUMMARY *Alexander Hamilton and Thomas Jefferson had different ideas about what was best for the country. Their disagreements led to America's first party system.*

ACCESS

What is a political party? How many political parties can you think of? When George Washington took office, the United States did not have any political parties. He thought they caused conflict. Copy the main idea map from page 8 into your history journal. In the largest circle, put *Hamilton and Jefferson's Disagreements*. As you read the chapter, write an issue they disagreed about in each of the smaller circles.

WORD BANK

Federalist   liberal   credit   interest   Democratic-Republican   capitalist   collateral   invest   conservative   capital   bond   free enterprise system

Choose words from the word bank to complete the sentences. One word is not used at all.

1. Thomas Jefferson was the leader of the _____ party.

2. If you borrow money, you must pay _____.

3. A capitalist system is sometimes called a _____.

4. A _____ favors civil liberties, democratic reforms and the use of governmental power to promote social progress.

5. The _____ party consisted of Alexander Hamilton's supporters.

6. When people get a loan, sometimes they must provide _____.

7. A _____ is a written promise to pay back a loan.

8. Many farmers and solders decided to _____ in the new U.S. government.

9. A _____ is someone who is reluctant to make changes.

10. Another word for borrowing power is _____.

11. _____ is money, or any goods or assets that can be turned into money.

WORD PLAY

Identify two of the above terms that have similar meanings. Next identify two of the above terms that have opposite meanings. Write your answers below.

_____

CRITICAL THINKING COMPARE AND CONTRAST

The phrases below describe Alexander Hamilton and Thomas Jefferson. In your history journal, copy the Venn Diagram on page 9. Write *Hamilton* above one circle and *Jefferson* above the other circle. The phrases that apply to only one person go in that person's circle. The phrases that apply to both go in the area where the two circles connect.

wanted a free education amendment	had faith in ordinary people	fought for freedom of the press
concerned about balancing liberty and power	feared the masses	encouraged business and industry
wanted the government to pay off its debt	headed a major political party	
wanted aristocratic leaders to govern	feared a powerful government	

WORKING WITH PRIMARY SOURCES

Stephen Vincent Benét wrote a poem about one of the Founding Fathers.

He could handle the Nation's dollars	And scratch like a wildcat, too.
With a magic that's known to few,	And he yoked the States together
He could talk with the wits and scholars	With a yoke that is strong and stout.

Who is the subject of the poem? Which lines reveal the person's identity? Circle your answers in the poem.

CHAPTER 4

A CAPITAL CITY

SUMMARY *The capital of the United States was moved to Washington, D.C., where the President's House and the Capitol were built.*

ACCESS

What are your favorite buildings? Have you ever wondered when they were built? Copy the sequence of events chart from page 9 into your history journal. As you read the chapter, write down the different events that occurred in the building of the U.S. capital.

WORD BANK   capital   Capitol

Choose words from the word bank to complete the sentence.

1. While touring the _____ city, George walked passed the _____ building.

WITH A PARENT OR PARTNER

The word *capital* has many different meanings. Write as many different meanings for the word capital as you can think of in five minutes. For extra fun, ask a parent or family member or partner to do the same. Compare lists by reading aloud. Use a dictionary or a thesaurus to learn any meanings that you did not include on your lists.

COMPREHENSION

How did each of the following people contribute to the building of the nation's capital? Answer in your history journal.

1. Major Andrew Ellicott

2. Benjamin Banneker

3. Pierre Charles L'Enfant

4. James Hoban

5. William Thornton

List two other people who contributed to the building of Washington, D.C.

WORKING WITH PRIMARY SOURCES

When describing Benjamin Banneker, a Quaker abolitionist wrote:

. . . the powers of the mind are disconnected with the colour of the skin.

In your own words, describe what this statement means. Write your response in your history journal.

WRITING

Imagine that it is 200 years ago. You are writing a travel guide for tourists who want to visit the new capital. Write a description of the highlights of Washington, D.C., in your history journal.

CHAPTER 5

COUNTING NOSES

SUMMARY *The census of 1790 counted nearly 4 million people living in the United States. In the following years, the population of the new nation would increase rapidly.*

ACCESS

What do you know about the census? Chances are, you were counted in the last one taken by the U.S. government. In your history journal, copy the K-W-L graphic organizer from page 8. In the "Know" column, write three things that you know about the U.S. census. Then, skim through the chapter and look at illustrations and maps. Fill in the second column with questions and things you want to find out about the census. Fill in the third column with information that you learned while reading the chapter.

WORD BANK   census   inhabitants

Choose a word from the word bank to complete the sentence.

1. Ohio had 45,000 _____ in 1803.

Look up the word that you did not use in the dictionary. Write a sentence using that word.

_____

MAP

Turn to page 34 of your book and look at the map.

1. Which state had the largest population in 1790? _____

2. How many people lived in that state? _____

3. Which states had fewer than 100,000 people in 1790? _____

WORKING WITH PRIMARY SOURCES

A French visitor to the U.S. described a frontiersman as

> a highly civilized being, who concentrates for a time to inhabit the backwoods, and who penetrates the wilds of the New World with the Bible, an axe, and some newspapers.

1. Is this assessment positive or negative? Write the reasons for your answer in your history journal.

2. In 1800 America's frontier region was west of the Appalachian Mountains. How does the French visitor describe this area? Write your answer in your history journal.

WRITING

In chapter 5, you read about the death of Ben Franklin. Imagine you are at Ben Franklin's yard sale. On a table, you see the following things: a candle, a kite, a pair of bifocals, a mailbox, a copy of *The Poor Richard's Almanack*, and a loaf of French bread. Write a short skit between you and Ben Franklin, where you ask him how he got all of those things and have him tell you where they came from. Include as many items as you can.

THE ADAMS FAMILY MOVES TO WASHINGTON

SUMMARY *The second president, John Adams, and his wife moved into the President's House in the newly built capital city. George Washington's death plunged the nation into mourning.*

ACCESS

You have probably seen the White House in pictures or on the television. How much do you know about the President's House, where John and Abigail Adams lived? Make a chart with two columns in your history journal. The first column should be called "What I Know." Write everything you know about the White House today. The second column should be called "What I Learned." After you read the chapter, write everything you have learned about the history of the President's House. Share your chart with other students if you have the chance.

WORD BANK   Executive Mansion   Oval Office

Choose words from the word bank to complete the sentences.

1. People used to call the place where the president lived the _____.

2. The _____ is the best-known room in the White House.

WORD PLAY

Write a sentence using both of the words in the word bank.

_____

Write the sentence again using different words in place of the word bank words. Look through the chapter to find possible substitutes.

_____

CRITICAL THINKING MAKING INFERENCES

An inference is a conclusion you can make from facts or reasoning. The chapter describes the experiences of John and Abigail Adams after they moved to Federal City. Check off the phrases below that are inferences you could make about the nation's capital when the Adamses lived there.

_____ The buildings were newly built.

_____ The city attracted many tourists.

_____ It could be reached by boat.

_____ Many national monuments were in the city.

_____ It was the largest city in the nation.

_____ The members of Congress had been to the city.

_____ It was located near New England.

_____ George and Martha Washington lived in the city.

WRITING

Imagine that you could travel back in time and talk to Abigail Adams. Describe to her how the White House has changed since she was the First Lady. Write your description in your history journal.

ABOUT PRESIDENT ADAMS

SUMMARY *John Adams had many strong points and many weak points. As president, he kept the country out of war but failed to stop political divisions from growing.*

ACCESS

Think about an important political leader. That person has likely been widely praised and widely criticized. John Adams was both praised and criticized while he was president. Copy the main idea map from page 8. In the center circle, write *John Adams*. In each of the smaller circles, write one fact about him that you learn as you read the chapter. Then go back and label the facts P for those that earned praise and C for those that brought criticism.

WORD BANK   diplomat   republicanism   protocol

Choose words from the word bank to complete the sentence. One word is not used.

1. The _____ observed proper _____ by bowing before the king at the reception.

Look up the word that you did not use in the dictionary. Write a sentence using that word.

_____

WITH A PARENT OR PARTNER

One of the meanings of the suffix *ism* refers to a doctrine or theory. In five minutes, write all of the *ism* words you can think of that refer to a doctrine or theory. Ask a parent or partner to do the same. Then read your lists to each other. Look up in a dictionary any words either of you doesn't know.

CRITICAL THINKING FACT OR OPINION

The chapter contains many facts and opinions about John Adams. Make a two-column chart in your journal. Label one column *Fact* and the other column *Opinion*. Write each sentence below from the chapter in the column where it belongs.

1. ". . . you will love him if ever you become acquainted with him."

2. "He was 61 when he became president."

3. "John Adams was a Federalist."

4. "Adams was a fine person—honorable and thoughtful."

5. "John Adams was a great man, but he was just passable as president."

6. "Adams was away 385 days in four years as president."

7. "He spent too much time at home in Quincy, Massachusetts."

8. "He was the lawyer who defended the British soldiers after the Boston Massacre."

WORKING WITH PRIMARY SOURCES

John Adams once described himself in a letter to a friend:

> The times, Madam, have made a Strange Being of me, . . . an irritable Fiery Mortal . . . as proud as a Caesar. But an honest man in all and to the Death.

In your history journal:

1. Rewrite the above quote in your own words to describe Adams.

2. Write whether the qualities that Adams lists about himself are traits that you would like to see in a president today? Why or why not?

WRITING

Write a short essay comparing John Adams with George Washington. Describe their similarities and differences. You may want to organize your ideas first. Use the outline graphic organizer on page 8 to list two or more main ideas. Fill in the details in the lines under each main idea.

CHAPTER 8

ALIEN AND SEDITION: AWFUL AND SORRY

SUMMARY *The Federalists passed laws that restricted freedoms. Many Americans believed the laws were unconstitutional.*

ACCESS

In 1798 the Congress passed a set of laws. These laws were followed by a series of events. In your history journal, copy the sequence of events chart on page 9. In the first box write *Congress passes the Alien and Sedition Acts*. Fill in the boxes that follow with events you learn about in the chapter.

WORD BANK

Alien and Sedition Acts   checks and balances   excises

Choose words from the word bank to complete the sentences.

1. The three branches of government operate through _____.

2. The _____ increased political division within the U.S. in the late 1790s.

3. American colonists hated paying the British _____.

WORD PLAY

In your history journal, write sentences using the words *alien*, *sedition*, *checks*, and *balances*. Write a separate sentence for each word. Look in a dictionary or thesaurus to learn more about the meanings of the individual words.

WORKING WITH PRIMARY SOURCES

According to Article I of the Bill of Rights:

> Congress shall make no law respecting an establishment of religion, or prohibiting the free exercise thereof; or abridging the freedom of speech, or of the press; or the right of the people peaceably to assemble, and to petition the Government for a redress of grievances.

1. Whom does the article address?

2. List three specific activities that are protected by the article.

3. Why is a Bill of Rights important?

Record your answers in your history journal.

WRITING

The Alien and Sedition Act made lots of people very angry. One way they expressed their anger was through political cartoons like the one on page 47. In your history journal, draw a political cartoon, expressing disapproval of the Alien and Sedition Act.

CHAPTER 9

SOMETHING IMPORTANT: JUDICIAL REVIEW

SUMMARY *Chief Justice John Marshall initiated judicial review, which strengthened the power of the Supreme Court.*

ACCESS

What are the three branches of the U.S. government? In your history journal, list three advantages of having a government with three branches.

WORD BANK   judicial review

Read the sidebar definition of judicial review on page 50. Write a sentence using the word *judicial*. Write another sentence using the word *review*. Finally, write a sentence using the term *judicial review*.

TIMELINE

In your history journal, copy the timeline graphic organizer on page 9. Include the following dates on your timeline: 1798, 1799, 1800, 1803, and 1804. Read the chapter to learn what happened in each of those years. List each event in the box next to the year in which it happened.

WORKING WITH PRIMARY SOURCES

Read the following descriptions of John Marshall.

His manners are plain yet dignified.

. . . his habits were remarkable for modest plainness . . .

. . . only the character of his mind, which seemed to have no flaw, made his influence irresistible upon all who were brought within its reach, . . .

Pure in life, broad in mind . . .

. . . his good temper and unwearied patience are equally agreeable on the bench and in the study.

. . . this excellent and amiable man clung to one rooted prejudice: he detested Thomas Jefferson.

1. Circle John Marshall's positive qualities.

2. Put a square around his negative qualities.

3. Which of the above traits would you like to see in the judges of today? What traits would you add to this list?

WRITING

Suppose the judicial review had never been established. Think about how that would have affected the three branches of government. Write a brief essay in your history journal explaining how the U.S. would be different today without judicial review.

MEET MR. JEFFERSON

SUMMARY *In 1801 Thomas Jefferson became the third president of the United States. He was the first Democratic-Republican to hold that office.*

ACCESS

Thomas Jefferson had ideas that differed from those of the first two presidents. In your history journal, label one page *The Jefferson Administration*. Make two columns, one labeled *similar*, the other labeled *different*. As you read the chapter, note how Jefferson's administration was similar to and different from those of his predecessors.

WORD BANK   radical   protective tariff

Choose a word from the word bank to complete the sentence.

1. Because of the _____, clothes made in Great Britain were more expensive than those made in the U.S. Look up in a dictionary the word that you did not use. Write a sentence using that word.

_____

In your history journal, make a list of all the words you can think of that mean the opposite of the word you looked up. Use a thesaurus if you need help.

CRITICAL THINKING SEQUENCE OF EVENTS

The sentences below describe events that occurred during the presidency of Thomas Jefferson. Put them in order by writing numbers in the blanks next to each event. (Write "1" next to the earliest event, and so forth.)

a. _____ Jefferson spends $15 million on the Louisiana Purchase.

b. _____ Aaron Burr kills Alexander Hamilton in a duel.

c. _____ Jefferson is sworn in a president.

d. _____ Jefferson sends an expedition to explore the Louisiana Territory.

e. _____ Jefferson reads his inaugural address.

f. _____ Thomas Kennedy writes a poem about the big cheese John Leland sent to Jefferson.

WORKING WITH PRIMARY SOURCES

Jefferson spoke the following words during his inaugural address:

> Let us unite with one heart and one mind. Every difference of opinion is not a difference of principle . . . . We are all Republicans—we are all Federalists.

1. What point is Jefferson trying to make?

2. Rewrite each of the sentences in your history journal. Use your own words, but convey the same meaning as the original text.

WRITING

The year is 1801. Jefferson has just taken office as the first Democratic-Republican president. You, however, are a Federalist. Many of your friends are worried about the future of the nation. Write a letter to a Federalist friend explaining why he or she should remain loyal to the new president and his administration.

CHAPTER 11

MERIWETHER AND WILLIAM— OR LEWIS AND CLARK

SUMMARY *Meriwether Lewis and William Clark led an expedition through the Louisiana Territory to the Pacific Coast. On their trip they learned about the people, land, plants, and animals of the West.*

ACCESS

You have probably heard the names Lewis and Clark. How much do you know about the trip they took over 200 years ago? In your history journal, copy the K-W-L chart from page 8. In the first column write everything you know about Lewis and Clark. Then, skim through the chapter and look at illustrations and maps. Fill in the second column with questions and things you want to find out about them. After you read the chapter, write down five new things that you learned about the Lewis and Clark expedition.

WORD BANK   Northwest Passage

1. Find the sentence that describes the term in the word bank. Write the definition of Northwest Passage.

2. Look up the word northwest in the dictionary. Write a sentence using the word.

3. Look up the word passage in the dictionary. Write a sentence using the word.

MAP

Look at the map on pages 60-61 of your book.

1. From which city did Lewis and Clark start their expedition?

2. On which two rivers did Lewis and Clark travel?

3. Why is part of the map shaded yellow?

4. What large body of water did Lewis and Clark reach?

Find the Western US Relief Map at the back of this book. Title the map *Lewis and Clark* and add them to the legend. Draw their route on the map and lable the following:

St. Louis   Missouri River

Fort Mandan   Rocky Montains

Mississippi River   Pacific Ocean

Columbia River   Fort Clatsop

WORKING WITH PRIMARY SOURCES

Reread Jefferson's instructions to Lewis on page 59 of your book.

1. What are five things that Jefferson wanted Lewis to learn about on his trip?

2. How was Lewis supposed to record his observations?

3. If Lewis and Clark were traveling today into an unknown land, how would they record their observations?

Record your answers in your history journal.

WRITING

Suppose you are a newspaper reporter who met Lewis and Clark after they returned from their trip. In your history journal, write down five questions that you would like to ask them for an article you will be writing about their expedition. Write down the answers you think Lewis and Clark would have given.

CHAPTER 12

AN ORATOR IN A RED JACKET SPEAKS

SUMMARY *When Christian missionaries sought to convert the Iroquois, their leader Sagoyewatha gave a speech asking white people to respect the Indians' religion and way of life.*

ACCESS

In your history journal, copy the main idea map graphic organizer from page 8. In the largest circle, put *Sagoyewatha*. In the smaller circles, write facts that you learn about Sagoyewatha as you read the chapter. When you've finished, write three adjectives you would choose to describe Sagoyewatha.

WORD BANK   orator   incorporate   convert

Choose words from the word bank to complete the sentences.

1. Red Jacket's skill as a speaker earned him a reputation as a great _____.

2. Thomas Jefferson wanted to _____ Indians into American society.

WITH A PARENT OR PARTNER

Look up the word orator in the dictionary. In your history journal, make a list of all the words you can think of that mean the same as orator. Ask a parent or partner to do the same. Then read your lists to each other. Who is your favorite orator? Ask your parent or partner the same question. Discuss your answers.

CRITICAL THINKING   DRAWING INFERENCES

After reading the chapter, what can you infer about the Iroquois and the Americans? Place a check next to each statement that is a valid inference.

_____ The Christian missionaries believed their religion was superior to that of the Iroquois.

_____ In 1805 the Iroquois tribes had a stronger military than the United States.

_____ Most Americans respected the Iroquois' right to freedom of religion.

_____ The earliest white settlers of North America relied upon the Indians for help.

_____ Religion was important to the Iroquois.

_____ Most Iroquois believed they had been treated fairly by white Americans.

WORKING WITH PRIMARY SOURCES

When speaking to Christian missionaries, Sagoyewatha described the history of relations between white settlers and the Indians. In your history journal, answer the questions that follow.

> The white people, brother, had now found our country. Tidings were carried back and more came amongst us. Yet we did not fear them. We took them to be friends. They called us brothers. We believed them . . . . At length their numbers had greatly increased. They wanted more land; they wanted our country. Our eyes were opened and our minds became uneasy. Wars took place. Indians were hired to fight against Indians, and many of our people were destroyed. They also brought strong liquor amongst us. It was strong and powerful and has slain thousands.

1. How did the Indians respond to the first white settlers of North America?

2. What caused conflict between the Indians and white people?

3. How did white people gain the upper hand in their fight against the Indians?

THE GREAT TEKAMTHI, ALSO CALLED TECUMSEH

SUMMARY *The growing American population threatened to take away more Indian lands. Tekamthi and his brother, Tenskwatawa, sought to unite the Indian tribes against the Americans.*

ACCESS

Tekamthi was a great leader who lived two centuries ago. Imagine that you could interview him. Before reading, skim through the chapter. To skim means to look over the pages quickly, noticing names, places, events, pictures and captions, and short features in the sidebars. Then in your history journal, make a list of five questions you would ask Tekamthi. One question might be "What are your religious beliefs?" Now read the chapter carefully and write the answers to the questions as you imagine Tekamthi might answer them.

WORD BANK   Shakers   shaman

Choose a word from the word bank to complete the sentence.

1. The _____ were a Christian group that used dances in worship services.

In a dictionary, look up the word that you did not use. Write a sentence using that word.

_____

MAP

Turn to page 71 of your book and look at the map. Answer the following questions in your history journal.

1. Where was Tecumseh born?

2. What do the red arrows on the map indicate?

3. Which lands did the Spanish control?

4. Who controlled the area in which Tecumseh died?

CRITICAL THINKING   COMPARE AND CONTRAST

The phrases below describe Tekamthi and Tenskwatawa. In your history journal, copy the Venn diagram on page 9. Write *Tekamthi* above one circle and *Tenskwatawa* above the other circle. The phrases that apply to only one person go in that person's circle. The phrases that apply to both go in the area where the two circles connect.

also called "The Prophet"	fought against the Americans in battle
wanted Indians to be proud of their heritage	muscular and handsome
a shaman	a Shawnee leader
born under a shooting star	defeated at Tippecanoe
a great warrior	his name means "The Panther Passing Across"

WRITING

Imagine that you are a teacher writing a report card for Tekamthi while he was still a boy. Begin like this: "Tekamthi is a natural leader. His classmates look up to him." Continue the report in your history journal.

OSCEOLA

SUMMARY *The Creeks divided into two groups—one group supported the Americans and the other group opposed the Americans. After the Red Sticks were forced into Florida, a leader named Osceola rose up among the Creeks.*

ACCESS

You have learned about several Native American groups thus far. Osceola was a leader of the Creeks. Copy the main idea map graphic organizer from page 8. In the center circle, write *Creeks*. In each of the smaller circles, write one fact about the tribe that you learn as you read the chapter.

WORD BANK   White Sticks   Red Sticks

Choose words from the word bank to complete the sentences.

1. The _____ were Creeks who supported Tecumseh.

2. Creeks who sided with the Americans were called _____.

Look up the word stick in a thesaurus. How many words did you find? The word stick is used as a noun in the word bank. Which of the words that you found in the thesaurus could be substituted for stick in the word bank?

_____

COMPREHENSION

Record your answer in your history journal.

1. Where did the Creeks live prior to the War of 1812?

2. Where did the Creeks live after the War of 1812?

3. Where did the Seminoles live?

4. Why do you think the Seminoles welcomed the Creeks after they were forced to move?

5. Why did the Creeks move?

WRITING

Reread the description from page 75 of a very popular Native American game. Can you draw a picture based on the description? In your history journal, draw the playing field and some of the players.

CHAPTER 15

THE REVOLUTIONARY WAR PART II, OR THE WAR OF 1812

SUMMARY *The U.S. and Britain fought another war from 1812 to 1815. After several battles, some victories and some defeats, the Americans had successfully defended their independence.*

ACCESS

Many important events occurred during the War of 1812. In your history journal, make a timeline of the war. Use the timeline graphic organizer on page 9 as a model. As you read the chapter, fill in the timeline with the major events of the War of 1812.

WORD BANK

War Hawks   John Bull   anthem

Choose words from the word bank to complete the sentences.

1. During the War of 1812, Francis Scott Key wrote a poem that later became the national _____.

2. _____ is the symbol of England.

3. Many young American leaders wanted to fight Britain. In 1812, these _____ convinced James Madison that war was necessary.

MAP

Look at the map on page 77 of your book. Answer the following questions in your history journal.

1. Which side won the Battle of Chrysler's Farm?

2. Who helped the British at the Battle of Fort Dearborn?

3. How many American victories are listed on the map?

4. What do the red lines in the Atlantic Ocean represent?

5. Where did the battles in the War of 1812 occur?

Find the Eastern US Relief map at the back of this book. Title it "The War of 1812" and add icons for the following to the legend: British blockade, british victories, US victories. Label the following on the map:

New Orleans	Bladensburg	Washington, DC
Fort McHenry	Chateaugay	Chrysler's Farm
Toronto	Buffalo	Put-in-Bay
Frenchtown	Fort Dearborn	Atlantic Ocean
Gulf of Mexico		

WORKING WITH PRIMARY SOURCES

Reread "Our National Anthem: The Star-Spangled Banner" on page 83 of your book. Answer the following questions in your history journal.

1. What specific object is the star-spangled banner?

2. Why are Americans most familiar with the first stanza of "The Star-Spangled Banner?"

CHAPTER 16

THE OTHER *CONSTITUTION*

SUMMARY *When launched in 1797, the U.S.S.* Constitution *was the largest frigate in the world. Never defeated in battle, the ship became an enduring symbol of the U.S. Navy.*

ACCESS

The U.S.S. *Constitution* is perhaps the most famous warship in American history. What do you know about this famous ship? In your history journal, copy the K-W-L chart from page 8. In the first column, write everything you know about the U.S.S. *Constitution* (if you don't know anything, that's okay). Then, skim through the chapter and look at illustrations and maps. Fill in the second column with questions and things you want to find out about the ship. As you read the chapter, make notes in the third column that answer your questions.

WORD BANK   Barbary States   frigate   corsairs   bey

Choose words from the word bank to complete the sentences. One word is not used at all.

_____ from the _____ captured hundreds of Americans in the Mediterranean Sea. The

U.S. government had to pay a steep ransom to get the people back. The _____ of Tripoli wanted even more money.

He declared war on the U.S.

Look up in a dictionary the word you did not use. Write a sentence using that word in your journal.

TIMELINE

The U.S.S. *Constitution* has had a long and distinguished history. In your history journal, copy the timeline graphic organizer on page 9. Include the following dates on your timeline: 1797, 1804, 1812, 1830, 1844, 1897, and 1997. Read the chapter to learn which U.S.S. *Constitution* event occurred in each of those years. List each event in the box next to the year in which it happened.

WORKING WITH PRIMARY SOURCES

Reread Oliver Wendell Holmes's poem "Old Ironsides" on page 86 of your book.

Write answers to the following questions in your history journal.

1. How would you describe the author's feelings about the U.S.S. *Constitution*?

2. What does the author mean when he writes "The harpies of the shore shall pluck/ The eagle of the sea!"?

3. What does the author think would be fitting fate for the U.S.S. *Constitution*?

WRITING

What would it be like to sail aboard the U.S.S. *Constitution*? Try to imagine what a day as a sailor would be like. Would you defend the U.S. from the British navy, or fight off Barbary pirates? In your history journal, describe an exciting day aboard the U.S.S. *Constitution*.

CHAPTER 17
THAT GOOD PRESIDENT MONROE

SUMMARY *During the presidency of James Monroe, the U.S. adopted a more confident foreign policy.*

ACCESS

How do you assess the administration of a past president? To organize information about the Monroe presidency, use the outline graphic organizer on page 8. As you read the chapter, identify two or more main ideas that relate to Monroe's time as president (for example "personal qualities" and "politics"). Write these down on the lines labeled "Main Idea." Add any details about each main idea in the lines below.

WORD BANK   Monroe Doctrine   expansionist   isolationist

Choose words from the word bank to complete the sentences.

1. After the War of 1812, the United States adopted an _____ policy in Florida.

2. The _____ established America's foreign policy regarding Latin America.

Look up the word *doctrine* in a dictionary. Which of the definitions fits with the usage of the word in the term *Monroe Doctrine*? Look up the word *expansionist* in a dictionary. Was the Monroe Doctrine an expansionist policy? Why or why not?

CRITICAL THINKING   SEQUENCE OF EVENTS

The pairs of words below describe events during the Monroe presidency. Write "before" or "after" in the blanks to complete each sentence correctly.

1. John C. Calhoun became Secretary of War _____ the Missouri Compromise.

2. Andrew Jackson led an army into Florida _____ Spain sold the state to the U.S.

3. Monroe gave his "Monroe Doctrine" speech _____ Spain and Portugal lost their colonies in South and Central America.

4. Seminole Indians helped slaves _____ they fled to Florida.

5. Andrew Jackson captured two Seminole chiefs _____ his men raised a British flag on his ship.

6. The U.S. released Osceola _____ the First Seminole War.

WORKING WITH PRIMARY SOURCES

The United States was still a new nation when James Monroe was president. When describing his country, Monroe said:

We lack many things, but we possess the most precious of all—liberty!

1. What did the United States lack when Monroe was president? List five things in your history journal.

2. Why do you think Monroe considered liberty to be "most precious of all"?

Answer in your history journal.

WRITING

Write a short essay in your history journal comparing James Monroe with one of the four presidents who preceded him. Compare the individuals and their presidencies, noting important similarities and differences.

18 JQA VS. AJ

SUMMARY *John Quincy Adams was well prepared to be president, but many Americans opposed him after he took office.*

ACCESS

John Quincy Adams was the son of John Adams, the nation's second president. In your history journal, label one page *The Two Adams Presidents*. Make two columns, one labeled *similar*, the other labeled *different*. As you read the chapter, note how John Quincy Adams's administration was similar to and different from that of his father.

WORD BANK   diplomat

Look up the definition of diplomat in a dictionary. Write the word in a sentence.

_____

WITH A PARENT OR PARTNER

In five minutes, write all of the words you can think of that have a similar meaning as diplomat. Ask a parent or partner to do the same. Then read your lists to each other. Look up in a dictionary any words either of you doesn't know. Next, list five diplomats—past or present. Ask your parent or partner to do the same. Compare your lists.

WORKING WITH PRIMARY SOURCES

Turn to page 95 of your book and reread the letters of Elijah Fletcher. Answer these questions in your history journal.

1. In the first letter, how does Fletcher describe the landscape through which he traveled?

2. Which former U.S. president did Fletcher meet?

3. List three things Fletcher saw during his travels that you would not see today.

WRITING

The year is 1825 and you are one of John Quincy Adams's most trusted advisers. Suppose on the day of his inauguration, Adams asks you for your advice on how he can be an effective president. In your history journal, write what you would tell the new president.

HISTORY JOURNAL

Don't forget to share your history journal with your classmates, and ask if you can see what their journals look like. You might be surprised—and get some new ideas.

CHAPTER 19

A DAY OF CELEBRATION AND TEARS

SUMMARY *Both John Adams and Thomas Jefferson died on the 50th anniversary of the signing of the Declaration of Independence.*

ACCESS By 1826 the United States had entered a new era. The Revolutionary leaders had passed the torch of leadership to a new generation. Symbolizing this transition, the man who was president in 1826 was the son of one of the men who helped found the U.S. Who was he?

WORD BANK   creed

Look up the word *creed* in the dictionary. Use it in a sentence.

Now find the sentence on page 96 that uses this word. Rewrite the sentence using the definition instead of the word itself.

WITH A PARENT OR PARTNER

The United States has a creed. Aside from nations, what else can have a creed? In your history journal list as many answers to this question as you can think of. Ask a parent or partner to do the same. Then compare lists by reading aloud.

COMPREHENSION

1. Why did Americans hold celebrations on July 4, 1826?

2. Where did John Adams live in 1826?

3. Where did Thomas Jefferson live in 1826?

4. Why were Adams and Jefferson unable to attend the July 4 celebrations?

WORKING WITH PRIMARY SOURCES

In 1826 John Adams wrote the following words about the nation he helped to found, the United States.

> A memorable epoch in the annals of the human race, destined in future history, to form the brightest or the blackest page according to the use or the abuse of these political institutions by which they shall, in time to come, be shaped by the human mind.

1. Look up the word *epoch* in a dictionary. What does it mean?

2. What is Adams worried about?

3. What is Adams calling on the American people to do?

Record your answers in your history journal.

WRITING

Suppose that John Adams and Thomas Jefferson attended the same anniversary celebration on July 4, 1826. What do you think they would have said to each other? In your history journal, write a dialogue that might have occurred between Adams and Jefferson on that special day.

CHAPTER 20

OLD HICKORY

SUMMARY *In 1828 Andrew Jackson became the first non-aristocrat to be elected president of the United States. His election strengthened democracy in America.*

ACCESS

Andrew Jackson was an important president. What do you know about his presidency? Copy the main idea map from page 8. Write Andrew Jackson's name in the center circle. In each of the smaller circles, write one fact that you learn about his presidency as you read the chapter.

WORD BANK   Old Hickory   spoils system   Old Ironsides

Choose words from the word bank to complete the sentences.

1. When he was a military commander, Jackson was called _____ by his men.

2. As president, Jackson started the _____ by giving government jobs to his supporters.

TIMELINE

In your history journal, copy the timeline graphic organizer on page 9. Write "Major events in Andrew Jackson's life" as your timeline title. On the date line, write the dates 1767, 1780, 1788, 1815, 1829, and 1833. Write the following phases in the event box next to the date they occurred.

Joins the South Carolina militia	Leads troops to victory at the Battle of New Orleans
Becomes the first U.S. president to ride on a train	Is appointed attorney general for the Tennessee region
Born in a log cabin	Is inaugurated president of the United States

If you get stuck, you may wish to review Chapter 15 of your book for a clue.

CRITICAL THINKING   FACT OR OPINION

A fact is a statement that can be proven. An opinion judges things or people, but it cannot be proved or disproved. Make a two-column chart in your journal. Label one column "Fact" and the other column "Opinion." Write each statement about Andrew Jackson in the column where it belongs.

1. Andrew Jackson was shot in the arm during a battle.

2. At 14 Andrew Jackson was an orphan.

3. Jackson was a barbarian and a savage.

4. The presidency became stronger because of Andrew Jackson.

5. Jackson received an honorary degree from Harvard University.

6. Chaos reigned in American politics during Jackson's presidency.

7. Jackson was the first president who was not from Massachusetts or Virginia.

8. The inauguration celebration at the White House was a disaster.

WRITING

Imagine you are a newspaper reporter in Washington, D.C., in 1829. You have been assigned to cover the Jackson inauguration. Write an article describing the event. Explain what you think Jackson's election means for America.

CHAPTER 21

YANKEE INGENUITY: COTTON AND MUSKETS

SUMMARY *Technological innovations created a factory-based system of production in America. This industrial revolution sparked the growth of a capitalist market economy.*

ACCESS

What is your favorite clothing store? Where do the clothes you like to buy at the store come from? In the 18th century, most people in America had to make their own clothes. This would change in the 1800s. In your history journal, use the K-W-L graphic organizer on page 8. In the first column, write down anything you might know about the Industrial Revolution in America. Then, skim through the chapter and look at illustrations and maps. Fill in the second column with questions and things you want to find out about this topic. As you read the chapter, make notes in the third column that answer your questions in the second column.

WORD BANK

| Industrial Revolution | cotton gin | market revolution |
| market economy | interchangeable parts | farm economy |

Fill in the paragraph with words from the word bank.

Soon after achieving independence, the U.S. experienced major economic changes. Americans learned how to use

machines to produce goods. This led to an _____. New ideas and inventions transformed the American

economy. For example, Eli Whitney invented the _____, which boosted cotton production. Whitney

later started making muskets with _____. Many new factories were built. The factory system led to

a _____. In this revolution, the U.S. went from a _____ to a _____.

WORKING WITH PRIMARY SOURCES

Before the factory system, people had to make their own clothes at home. Lucy Larcom did not like to do this.

> I think it must have been at home, while I was a small child, that I got the idea that the chief end of woman was to make clothing for mankind. . . . I suppose I have to grow up and have a husband and put all those little stitches into his coats and pantaloons. Oh, I never, never can do it!

Answer the following questions in complete sentences. Record your answers in your history journal.

1. Based on this passage, how do you think Lucy felt about the growth of factories that could produce clothes quickly and efficiently?

2. Read the paragraph about Lucy at the top of page 109. How do you think Lucy felt about working in a factory?

3. Do you think that working in a factory changed Lucy's opinion about making clothes at home? Why or why not?

WRITING

Suppose the Industrial Revolution did not reach the United States in the early 1800s. How would that have changed the development of the nation? Write a brief essay in your history journal explaining how U.S. history would have been different without industrialization.

CHAPTER 22

GOING PLACES

SUMMARY *In the early 1800s Americans built new roads and canals to improve cross-country transportation.*

ACCESS

"One thing leads to another." Have you ever heard that saying? On a broad scale, the Industrial Revolution led to a transportation revolution in America. In your history journal, copy the cause and effect chart on page 9. As you read the chapter, identify three developments that improved transportation. Write these down in the "Effect" column. Next, identify a cause for each of the developments (or effects). Write these in the "Cause" column.

WORD BANK   corduroy   macadam   pike   lock   celeripede   aqueduct

Choose words from the word bank to complete the sentences. Two words are not used at all.

1. In the early 1800s the _____, an early type of bicycle, appeared in the U.S.

2. Of the new roads that were being built, the best were _____ roads.

3. Travelers had to pay a toll to get the gatekeeper to move the _____ barrier.

4. Workers laid logs side by side to build a _____ road.

CRITICAL THINKING   SEQUENCE OF EVENTS

The sentences below list events relating to the transportation revolution in America. Use numbers to put them in the correct order (use "1" for the first event, and so on).

_____ The National Road reached Wheeling, West Virginia.

_____ A ton of grain could be shipped on the Erie Canal for $8.

_____ Benjamin Franklin suggested that canals should be used to move goods and people.

_____ Work began on the Erie Canal.

_____ The celeripede appeared in America.

_____ The National Road reached Columbus, Ohio.

WORKING WITH PRIMARY SOURCES

Turn to page 112 and reread Charles Fenno Hoffman's description of the National Road. Answer the following questions in your history journal.

1. What covers the surface of the road?

2. How does Hoffman assess the early construction of the road?

3. What does Hoffman think is the best feature of the National Road?

TEAKETTLE POWER

SUMMARY *Inventors built engines that ran on steam power. Steamboats and railroads greatly improved transportation in America.*

ACCESS

Timelines can help you understand how events in history are connected. In your history journal, copy the timeline graphic organizer on page 9. Include the following dates on your timeline: 1800, 1810, 1820, 1830, 1840, 1850, and 1860. As you read the chapter, note the important events in the history of steamboats and railroads. Place these events in the appropriate locations on the timeline.

WORD BANK   iron horses   locomotives   steam power   horsepower

Choose words from the word bank to complete the sentences. One word is not used at all.

1. The first real _____ appeared in England, after George Stephenson built the Rocket in 1828.

2. People in the 1800s called trains "teakettles on tracks" and _____.

3. _____ made traveling upriver much faster.

Look up in a dictionary the word that you did not use. Write a sentence using that word in your journal.

MAP

Study the map on pages 122-123 of your book. Answer in your history journal.

1. The map shows America in which year?

2. What do the red lines on the map represent?

3. Which part of the country were most of the railroads located?

4. If you wanted to ship goods from Lake Erie to the Ohio River, what would you use?

5. What does the pink shaded area on the map represent?

CRITICAL THINKING   COMPARE AND CONTRAST

The phrases below relate to steamboats and railroads. In your history journal, copy the Venn diagram graphic organizer on page 9. Write "Steamboats" above one circle and "Railroads" above the other circle. Write the phrases that apply to only one form of transportation in the appropriate circle. The phrases that apply to both forms of transportation go in the area where the two circles connect.

Relied on steam power	The *North River* was an early example
Could travel at 30 miles per hour	Baltimore & Ohio
Changed transportation in America	Traveled up the Mississippi River
George Stephenson was an important inventor	Robert Fulton was an important inventor
First appeared in England	Relied on tracks

WRITING

Suppose you were alive in the early 1800s. Pretend that you have just seen a locomotive for the first time. What does it look like? What do you hear and smell? Try to imagine the awe that such machines inspired in people during that time period. Write a poem describing the locomotive.

MAKING WORDS

SUMMARY *Though Cherokees created a written language and adopted white culture, the U.S. government forced them to give up their land and move west.*

ACCESS

To organize the information in chapter 24, use the outline graphic organizer on page 8. As you read the chapter, identify two or more main ideas that relate to Sequoyah and the Cherokees (for example "Creating a Written Language" and "Removal"). Write these down on the lines labeled "Main Idea." Add any details about each main idea in the lines below.

WORD BANK   Indian Removal Act

1. Find the sentence that describes the term in the word bank. Write the definition of *Indian Removal Act*.

_____

2. Look up the word *removal* in the dictionary. Write a sentence using the word.

_____

MAP

Turn to page 128 of your book and look at the map. Answer in your history journal.

1. The map covers which years in American history?

2. The map shows where several different Indian nations once lived. Which nation lived in the modern-day state of North Carolina? (look at a modern U.S. map if you need help)

3. What were the different Indian nations forced to do?

4. List two modern-day states that were once part of the area labeled "Indian Territory?"

CRITICAL THINKING   DRAWING CONCLUSIONS

Place a check mark in front of each statement that is a valid conclusion that can be drawn from the information in the chapter.

_____ 1. The Cherokees did not have the military strength to resist the U.S. government.

_____ 2. Indians were unable to learn how to read.

_____ 3. President Jackson believed Indians should have the same rights as U.S. citizens.

_____ 4. Most Americans did not respect the Cherokees' claim to the land on which they lived.

_____ 5. It was possible for children to learn the language Sequoyah created.

_____ 6. Sequoyah approved of the Indian Removal Act.

_____ 7. The discovery of gold in Georgia increased the pressure on Cherokees to leave their land.

WORKING WITH PRIMARY SOURCES

Sequoyah's friends did not want him to create a written language. They told him to stop. Sequoyah responded by saying:

> If our people think I am making a fool of myself, you may tell our people that what I am doing will not make fools of them. They did not cause me to begin and they shall not cause me to give up.

Write answers to the following questions in your history journal.

1. Is the statement Sequoyah makes in the first sentence correct? Explain why or why not?

2. Is the statement Sequoyah makes in the second sentence correct? Who did cause him to begin?

WRITING

Imagine that you are a newspaper reporter who has been granted an interview with Sequoyah. In your history journal, make a list of five questions you would ask him. One question might be "Why does the language system you invented contain 86 symbols?" Write the answers to the questions as you imagine Sequoyah might answer them.

A TIME TO WEEP

SUMMARY *Ignoring a Supreme Court ruling, the U.S. government forced several Indian nations to leave their land and move west of the Mississippi River.*

ACCESS

There are many dark events in U.S. history. In Chapter 25 you will learn about one of the darkest of these events. Copy the main idea map from page 8 into your history journal. In the largest circle, write *Trail of Tears*. In each of the smaller boxes, write one fact that you learn as you read the chapter.

WORD BANK   Trail of Tears

1. Look up the word *trail* in a dictionary. Use the word in a sentence.

_____

2. Look up the word *tears* in the dictionary. Write a sentence using the word.

_____

3. What is the significance of the phrase "Trail of Tears"? Record your answer in your journal.

TIMELINE

Match the events in the right column with the dates in the left column. A date may match up with more than one event.

1831	The Creeks are forced to move west.
1832	Black Hawk leads a campaign to regain the Sauk and Fox homelands.
1834	The Cherokees are forced to move west.
1836	John Marshall rules in the *Barron* v. *Baltimore* case.
1838	The Choctaws are forced to move west.
	The Chickasaws are forced to move west.
	Henry Clay runs for president against Andrew Jackson.

COMPREHENSION

Reread the discussion of the *Worcester* v. *Georgia* case in Chapter 25. Answer the following questions in complete sentences. Record your answers in your history journal.

1. What was Samuel Worcester's occupation?

2. What was Worcester unable to get in Georgia?

3. Who was the chief justice of the Supreme Court who ruled on the case?

4. The Supreme Court decided in favor of which side?

5. How did President Andrew Jackson respond to the decision?

WRITING

The Cherokees used the U.S. court system to try to keep their land. Suppose you are one of the Cherokee lawyers arguing the case. In your history journal, write an argument defending the Cherokees' claim to their land.

THE SECOND SEMINOLE WAR

SUMMARY *Osceola led Seminole warriors in a war of resistance against Americans in Florida.*

ACCESS

The sequence of events graphic organizer is a good way to understand the Second Seminole War. Copy the chart on p. 9 into your history journal. In the first box, write "Americans pressure the Seminoles to leave their lands in Florida." Fill in the boxes that follow as you connect events. The result box should contain a fact from the final page of the chapter.

WORD BANK   homesteaders   guerrilla bands

Choose words from the word bank to complete the sentences.

1. Seminole warriors divided into _____ to fight the Americans.

2. _____ wanted land in Florida and called for the removal of the Indians living there.

WORD PLAY   Write a sentence that includes both terms from the word bank.

_____

The core of a word is a smaller word or group of letters within the word. What is the core word of *homesteader*? Write a sentence using the core word.

_____

CRITICAL THINKING   CAUSE AND EFFECT

Match the "causes" in the left column with the "effects" in the right column.

1. General Jesup could not defeat Osceola,	a. SO the Seminoles did not want to live with them.
2. American homesteaders wanted land in Florida,	b. SO he called for his family to be with him.
3. The White Sticks had fought against Indians,	c. SO they demanded that the Seminoles move away.
4. The Seminole War cost many American lives,	d. SO he violated a flag of truce to capture him.
5. Osceola's malaria grew worse in prison,	e. SO the Second Seminole War ended.
6. The U.S. stopped fighting the Seminoles in 1842,	f. SO it became unpopular with the American people.

WORKING WITH PRIMARY SOURCES

Reread the statement by Opothleyoholo, below. Then respond to these questions in complete sentences.

> Our people yet abhor the idea of leaving all that is dear to them—the graves of their relatives; but circumstances have changed their opinions; they have become convinced of their true situation; that they cannot live in the same field with the white man. Our people have done that which we did not believe they would have done at the time we made the treaty; they have sold their reservations—it is done and cannot now be helped; the white man has taken possession, and has every advantage over us; it is impossible for the red and white man to live together.

1. How do the Indians feel about leaving their land?

2. Why did the Indians sell their reservations?

3. Reread the last sentence in the quote. Do think Opothleyoholo was correct when he made that statement in 1835? Why or why not?

WRITING

What do you think would have happened if Osceola had not been captured by General Jesup? In your history journal, describe how you think the Second Seminole War would have ended if Osceola had escaped capture.

HISTORY'S PARADOX

SUMMARY *Though America's national creed promised liberty and equality for all, millions of people were enslaved in the United States.*

ACCESS

In this chapter you will learn about a paradox in American history. In your history journal, label one page *The American Paradox*. Make two columns, one labeled *America's Declared Principles*, the other labeled *The Reality of Slavery*. Fill in the columns with facts as you learn about how slavery violated America's national creed.

WORD BANK   hypocrisy   bigotry

Choose words from the word bank to complete the sentences.

1. _____ was widespread among those Americans who denied liberty to other people based on the color

   of their skin.

2. The Founders who promised equal rights for all, yet defended the institution of slavery, were guilty of _____.

3. What do you call a person who practices hypocrisy? Write a sentence using that word.

_____

4. What do you call a person who practices bigotry? Write a sentence using that word.

_____

CRITICAL THINKING MAKING INFERENCES

America's Founders wrote about liberty and equality in the Declaration of Independence and the Constitution. Yet, reality was different for many Americans. Check off the phrases below that describe scenes that were likely to happen in the United States in the 1800s.

_____ a slave votes for president

_____ a slave decides to work for another master

_____ a master abuses a slave

_____ a slave receives a fair trial by jury

_____ white people hunt for a runaway slave

_____ a white person is arrested in 1810 for importing a slave from Africa

_____ a slave is sold and separated from his wife

_____ a black person owns slaves

_____ a child becomes a slave at birth

_____ a white person calls for the end of slavery

_____ a slave is elected to Congress

WORKING WITH PRIMARY SOURCES

The quote below is from an article in a Maryland newspaper.

> Though our bodies differ in color from yours; yet our souls are similar in a desire for freedom. [Difference] in color . . . can never constitute a [difference] in rights. Reason is shocked at the absurdity! Humanity revolts at the idea! . . . Why then are we held in slavery? . . . Ye fathers of your country; friends of liberty and of mankind, behold our chains! . . . To you we look up for justice—deny it not—it is our right.

1. Whom do you think the writer is addressing?

2. What does the writer mean by the statement: "Reason is shocked at the absurdity!"

3. What does the writer want to change?

WRITING

The title of Chapter 27 is "History's Paradox." A paradox is a

    contradiction   solution   dream   ferocious animal

Circle your answer. In your history journal, write about a paradox, past or present, in your life.

A MAN WHO DIDN'T DO AS HIS NEIGHBORS DID

SUMMARY *A few wealthy slave owners in the South, such as Robert Carter III and Henry Laurens, came to believe that slavery was wrong.*

ACCESS

Robert Carter III was a man of great wealth. Copy the main idea map from page 8. In the largest circle put *Carter*. In each of the smaller circles, write one fact about Carter that you learn as you read the chapter.

WORD BANK   established church   emancipated   dissenting church   Age of Reason

Choose words from the word bank to complete the sentences.

1. The Anglican Church was the _____ in Virginia.

2. During the _____ people read more books and asked more questions.

3. Though Robert paid taxes to the Anglican Church, he attended services at a _____.

4. After realizing the error of his ways, the plantation owner _____ his slaves.

WITH A PARENT OR PARTNER

In your history journal, list all of the words you can think of that means the same as emancipate. Use a thesaurus if you need help. Ask a parent or family member of make a list too. Read your lists to each other. Look up in a dictionary any words either of you does not know.

CRITICAL THINKING   COMPARE AND CONTRAST

The phrases below describe Robert Carter III and Henry Laurens. In your history journal, copy the Venn diagram graphic organizer on page 8. Write *Carter* above one circle and *Laurens* above the other circle. The phrases that apply to only one person go in that person's circle. The phrases that apply to both go in the area where the two circles connect.

the wealthiest merchant in Charleston	owned many slaves
lived in a home called Nomini Hall	supported the Virginia Statute for Religious Freedom
believed slavery was wrong	imprisoned in the Tower of London
freed his slaves	became a deist, and then a Baptist
member of the Continental Congress	grandson of "King Robin"

WORKING WITH PRIMARY SOURCES

Robert Carter III wrote the following words in 1791:

> Whereas I Robert Carter of Nomini Hall in the County of Westmoreland & Commonwealth of Virginia [own] . . . many negroes & mulatto slaves . . . and Whereas I have for some time past been convinced that to retain them in Slavery is contrary to the true principles of Religion and justice. . . . I do hereby declare that such . . . shall be emancipated.

1. What does Carter mean when he writes that slavery "is contrary to the true principles of Religion and justice"?

2. What do you think happened to Carter's slaves after he made the above statement?

Record your answers in your history journal.

29 AFRICAN-AMERICANS

SUMMARY *African-Americans, both free and enslaved, called for an end to slavery.*

ACCESS

Slavery is one of the most shameful aspects of America's past. To organize information from this chapter, make a chart with two columns in your history journal. The first column should be called "What I Know." Write everything you already know about slavery in the United States. The second column should be called "What I Learned." After you read the chapter, fill in this column with what you have learned about slavery in the U.S.

WORD BANK   oppressions   pastor   auction

Choose words from the word bank to complete the sentences.

1. The _____ preached a sermon calling for an end to slavery.

2. A woman was sold at the _____, separating her from her husband and children.

3. African-Americans faced many _____ in the United States.

Try to think of words that have similar meanings as the words in the word bank. Write down three of the words that come to mind, one for each of the words in the word bank. Write a sentence using each of the new words.

CRITICAL THINKING CLASSIFICATION

Several different groups of people spoke out against slavery. Make a chart with three columns in your history journal. Label the columns *Free Blacks*, *Slaves*, and *Whites*. Write each of the names below in the correct column. Some individuals may be placed in two columns, reflecting a change of status that occurred.

Richard Allen	Marquis de Lafayette
Paul Cuffe	Quock Walker
James Madison	Elizabeth Freeman
Josiah Henson	George R. Allen
Moses Grandy	John Woolman

WORKING WITH PRIMARY SOURCES

Reread the sidebar passages on pages 146, 147, and 149 of your book.

Write responses to the following questions in your history journal.

1. What effect did slavery have on black families in the South?

2. How did those who were enslaved feel about their condition?

3. What do you think would have happened if every white person in America had observed a slave auction first-hand?

WRITING

The year is 1820. You are a newspaper reporter assigned to cover a slave auction in Charleston, South Carolina. In your history journal, write an article describing the event.

THE KING AND HIS PEOPLE

SUMMARY *Cotton was the foundation of the southern economy. Because plantations required many workers, cotton increased the value of slaves in the South.*

ACCESS

The chapter title refers to a king. This king ruled in the South. What was this king's name? Cotton. The K-W-L chart on page 8 will help you get the most from Chapter 30. Copy this chart into your history journal. In the first column write what you already know about cotton growing in the South in the first half of the 1800s. Then, skim through the chapter and look at illustrations and maps. Fill in the second column with questions and things you want to find out about this topic. After finishing the chapter, write in the third column what you learned about King Cotton.

WORD BANK   coffle   lynch   yeoman farmers

Choose words from the word bank to complete the sentences.

1. The plantation owner marched the _____ into town.

2. Most _____ in the South did not own slaves.

3. An angry mob decided to _____ the suspect, even though a trial had not been held.

WITH A PARENT OR PARTNER

The word lynch came into common usage because of the actions of a person, John Lynch. In your journal list as many words in the English language as you can think of that were originally the name of a real person (for example, "John Hancock" now means signature). Ask a parent or partner to make a list too. Then compare lists by reading aloud. Look up any new words in a dictionary.

COMPREHENSION

Review Chapter 30 and answer the following questions in your journal.

1. Mobs in Southern states lynched how many people between 1840 and 1860?

2. Which part of the Constitution prevented Congress from ending the slave trade prior to 1808?

3. What did both white and black Southerners like to do during their leisure time?

4. Name two famous plantation owners in the South.

5. Why do you think cotton was called "King" in the South?

WORKING WITH PRIMARY SOURCES   The passage below was a song sung by slaves.

> We raise the wheat,
> They give us the corn;
> We bake the bread,
> They give us the crust;
> We sift the meal,
> They give us the husk;
> We peel the meat,
> They give us the skin;
> And that's the way
> They take us in.

1. Whom does "They" refer to in the song?

2. The final line is "And that's the way/They take us in." What do you think that means?

WRITING

In your history journal, write a poem describing the South in the early 1800s.

31 ABOLITIONISTS WANT TO END SLAVERY

SUMMARY *Abolitionists stepped up their efforts to end slavery, increasing tensions between the North and the South.*

ACCESS

Abolitionists viewed slavery as evil. This caused them to take action. These actions, in turn, led others to act in opposition to the abolitionists. Copy the cause and effect chart on page 9. As you read the chapter, take notes on the fight against slavery, filling in the chart with "causes" that you learn about, and their "effects." In the first half of the 1800s the United States was divided. In some of the states, slavery was legal. In the other states it was illegal to own slaves. How did this situation come about?

WORD BANK   abolition   Missouri Compromise   secede

Choose words from the word bank to complete the sentences.

1. People in New England threatened to _____ from the United States.

2. The _____ left an equal number of free states and slave states in the Union.

3. William Lloyd Garrison published *The Liberator*, in which he called for the _____ of slavery.

Look up the word *secede* in a dictionary. What are the different forms of this word? Write two sentences. Each sentence should include a different form of the word *secede*.

_____

_____

CRITICAL THINKING   FACT OR OPINION

Make a two-column chart in your history journal. Label one column *Fact* and the other column *Opinion*. Write each sentence below from the chapter in the column where it belongs.

1. Two years later Franklin helped found the American Abolition Society.
2. Now the "Old South" was in decline.
3. Slavery is a moral evil in any society . . .
4. Then, in 1820, Missouri asked to enter the Union as a free state.
5. Former slaves began to speak out and tell their stories.
6. [Slavery] was a fine way of life—for slave and master.
7. Then Maine was made a nonslave state.
8. No good would come of this.

WORKING WITH PRIMARY SOURCES

In 1804 a slave was captured after taking part in a rebellion. At his trial he told the court:

> I have nothing more to offer than what George Washington would have had to offer had he been taken by the British and put to trial by them. I have adventured my life in endeavoring to obtain the liberty of my countrymen, and am a willing sacrifice to their cause.

1. What were the similarities between George Washington and this slave?

2. What is the slave saying in the second sentence? Rewrite it using your own words.

WRITING

Use the Internet or a library to learn more about Nat Turner, Denmark Vesey, and Gabriel Prosser. In your history journal, write a short biography of one of these three men.

FREDERICK DOUGLASS

SUMMARY *After escaping from slavery, Frederick Douglass traveled across the North speaking about his experiences. Douglass became one of the nation's best-known abolitionists.*

ACCESS

Frederick Douglass devoted his life to fighting for human rights for the oppressed. In your history journal, copy the main idea map graphic organizer from page 8. In the largest circle, write *Frederick Douglass*. In the smaller circles, write facts that you learn about Douglass as you read the chapter.

WORD BANK   freeman   slave catchers

Choose words from the word bank to complete the sentences.

1. _____ traveled throughout the northern states searching for slaves who had escaped.

2. For many years, the slave dreamed of living as a _____.

MAP

Turn to page 161 of your book and look at the map.

1. What does the orange shaded area on the map represent?

2. List three U.S. cities shown on the map.

3. The map shows the boundaries of the U.S. in 1830. Who was president that year?

4. List three current U.S. states that were not states in 1830.

5. What was the westernmost U.S. state in 1830? (Hint: it was also the state that had most recently joined the Union.)

CRITICAL THINKING   SEQUENCE OF EVENTS

The phrases below are events in the life of Frederick Douglass. Use numbers to put them in the correct order (use "1" for the first event, and so on).

_____ escapes to freedom   _____ becomes an adviser to Abraham Lincoln

_____ sent to Baltimore to be a companion to a white boy   _____ writes a book about his life as a slave

_____ becomes a speaker for the Massachusetts Anti-Slavery Society   _____ learns how to read

WORKING WITH PRIMARY SOURCES

The quotation below is from Frederick Douglass.

> People in general will say they like colored men as well as any other, but in their proper place. They assign us to that place; they don't let us do it ourselves nor will they allow us a voice in the decision. They will not allow that we have a head to think, and a heart to feel and a soul to aspire . . . . That's the way we are liked. You degrade us, and then ask why we are degraded—you shut our mouths and then ask why we don't speak—you close your colleges and seminaries against us, and then ask why we don't know more.

1. Whom is Douglass referring to with the word "you"?

2. Whom is Douglass referring to with the word "us"?

3. Summarize the above quote in a single sentence.

WRITING

Imagine that you have a chance to talk to Frederick Douglass. In your history journal, make a list of five questions you would like to ask him. Write the answers to your questions as you imagine Douglass might answer them.

33 NAMING PRESIDENTS

SUMMARY *None of the eight presidents who followed Andrew Jackson served more than one term in office. They are not as highly regarded as the first seven U.S. presidents.*

ACCESS

In Chapter 33 you will learn about a succession of U.S. presidents. In your history journal, copy the sequence of events graphic organizer. Add three more boxes to the chart. Write *Martin Van Buren* and the dates he served as president in the first box. As you read the chapter, fill in the other boxes with the names of the following presidents. Include the dates that each president served as well. For each president, list a significant fact about his administration.

WORD BANK   Free Soilers

Find the paragraph on page 164 in which this term appears. Reread the paragraph and complete the following sentence.

The main cause of the Free Soilers was _____

MAP

Study the map on page 164. Then, find the Blank US Political Map With State boundaries at the end of this book. Title this map *The US in 1850*, and recreate the map from page 164. Label the states and territories. Use the atlas at the back of your book to help you.

CRITICAL THINKING   CLASSIFICATION

Write down the names of the eight presidents you learned about in this chapter. Write each name on a separate line and skip a few lines between each name. Every phrase below relates to one of the eight presidents. Write each phrase under the name of the president to which it relates.

Referred to as "His Accidency"	Succeeded by Abraham Lincoln
The only bachelor president	"Old Rough and Ready"
"I am the hardest working man in the country."	Died of exhaustion three months after his term
First president to be born a U.S. citizen	Replaced Andrew Jackson
Was president for only 31 days	From New Hampshire
Whigs kicked him out of their party	Installed the first kitchen stove in the White House
Graduated from Bowdoin College	Second president to die in office
Sent Commodore Matthew Perry to Japan	Old Tippecanoe

WORKING WITH PRIMARY SOURCES

Andrew Jackson made the following statement about the man he appointed as minister to Russia.

> It was as far as I could send him out of my sight, and where he could do the least harm. I would have sent him to the North Pole if we had kept a minister there!

1. Jackson is referring to which person?

2. What does the statement tell you about how government appointments are made?

3. What does the statement tell you about U.S.-Russian relations in the 1830s?

WRITING

Suppose you could travel back in time to advise one of the eight presidents you learned about in this chapter. Which president would you choose? In your history journal, describe the advice you would give to him.

A TRIUMVIRATE IS THREE PEOPLE

SUMMARY *Daniel Webster, Henry Clay, and John C. Calhoun were three powerful leaders in Congress. Each was a great orator who spoke for the interests of his region of the United States.*

ACCESS

Make a four-column chart in your history journal. Label the columns *Webster, Clay, Calhoun,* and *Adams* (the Adams refers to John Quincy Adams). Write down three facts about each man that you learn as you read the chapter.

WORD BANK   triumvirate   oratory   tariff   Whig

Choose words from the word bank to complete the sentences.

1. Congress approved a _____ that increased the price of clothes made in Europe.

2. Senator Webster delivered an _____ that amazed everyone who heard it.

3. Henry Clay was the leader of the _____ Party, which formed to oppose Andrew Jackson.

4. John C. Calhoun, Henry Clay, and Daniel Webster formed a _____ in the Congress.

WITH A PARENT OR PARTNER

In your history journal, list all the English words you can think of that begin with the same first syllable as triumvirate. Ask a parent or partner to also make a list. Compare your lists. What does tri mean?

CRITICAL THINKING   COMPARE AND CONTRAST

The phrases below describe Henry Clay, Daniel Webster, and John C. Calhoun. Look at the model of a Venn diagram on page 9. Draw a three-circle Venn diagram in your history journal. Label the circles so that each represents one of the three men. Copy the phrases below in the correct circles. The phrases that apply to only one person go in that person's circle. The phrases that apply to two people go in the area where the two circles belonging to those people connect. Any phrases that relate to all three belong in the area formed by all three circles.

A U.S. senator	Represented a slave state
Supported Massachusetts shipowners	Andrew Jackson's vice president
Wanted to be president	A powerful speaker
Known as "the great compromiser"	Speaker of the House of Representatives
Defended the Southern way of life	A Yankee
Spoke out against slavery	Opposed the collection of tariffs

WORKING WITH PRIMARY SOURCES

One of the leaders you learned about in this chapter made the following statement:

> There never has yet existed a wealthy and civilized society in which one portion of the community did not . . . live on the labor of the other . . .

1. Who made the above statement?

2. What point is the person trying to make with the statement?

3. Do you believe the point is valid? Why or why not?

Record your answers in your history journal.

WRITING

Suppose you were in the Senate chamber on a day that Webster, Clay, or Calhoun spoke. Write a diary entry describing what you saw and heard.

35 THE GREAT DEBATE

SUMMARY *A great debate raged on the floor of the Senate over the issue of states' rights versus federal authority.*

ACCESS

To organize the information in this chapter, use the outline graphic organizer on page 8. As you read, identify two or more main ideas from the "The Great Debate." Write these down on the lines labeled "Main Idea." Add any details about each main idea in the lines below.

WORD BANK   secession   sovereign

Choose words from the word bank to complete the sentences. One word is used twice.

1. Unable to win the western senators to their side, southern leaders increasingly considered _____.

2. Senator Hayne said that the states were _____, while Senator Webster held that the people were

_____.

Look up in a dictionary both words from the word bank. Write one sentence that includes both words.

_____

CRITICAL THINKING   FACT OR OPINION

Facts are statements that can be proved. Opinions make judgments but cannot be proved or disproved. Make a two-column chart in your history journal. Label one column "Facts" and the other column "Opinions." Write each sentence below from the chapter in the column where it belongs.

1. Hayne is also a brilliant man, and a fine speaker.

2. Soon after his debate with Daniel Webster, Robert Hayne gives up his seat in the Senate to become governor of South Carolina.

3. Calhoun is appointed to replace Hayne.

4. We are not a Nation, but a Union, a confederacy of equal and sovereign states.

5. When men of high standing attempt to trample upon the rights of the weak, they are the fittest objects for example and punishment.

6. His arguments are clear and brilliant.

7. There isn't an empty seat in the Senate.

8. This same year (1830), in Philadelphia, Louis A. Godey begins publishing *Godey's Lady's Book*.

WORKING WITH PRIMARY SOURCES

The following quote is from Daniel Webster.

> The inherent right in the people to reform their government I do not deny. And they have another right, and that is to resist unconstitutional laws without overturning the government.

1. What does Webster mean by "inherent right"? Use a dictionary if you need help.

2. What are some ways that people can exercise the second right described by Webster?

Record your answers in your history journal.

WRITING

Write dialogue for a conversation about the Union that could have taken place between John C. Calhoun and Daniel Webster. Write lines that you imagine each person might have spoken.

LIBERTY FOR ALL

SUMMARY *Despite the serious problems that remained unsolved, Americans had made excellent progress toward achieving the goals set forth by their nation's Founders.*

ACCESS

In reading this book, you have learned about the early history of the United States. Reflect on what you have read thus far. How do you feel about the people and the nation that you learned about?

WORD BANK   extraordinary

Look up the word *extraordinary* in a dictionary. Find the sentence in Chapter 36 in which the word appears. Rewrite the sentence using the definition of the word. _____

_____

WITH A PARENT OR PARTNER

Review the chapters of your book. Make a list of people you learned about who you think were extraordinary. Ask a parent or partner to make a list of extraordinary Americans who lived between 1789 and 1850. Read your lists to each other. Explain why you think each person was extraordinary.

COMPREHENSION

1. Where did Abraham Lincoln move when he was 21?

2. How did Thomas Hart Benton view slavery?

3. Name one group in America that did not have equal rights in 1850.

This chapter lists several prominent Americans. Which of them do you expect to read more about in the next book?

WORKING WITH PRIMARY SOURCES

Andrew Jackson spoke the following words before he died:

> I expect to see you all in heaven, both white and black.

1. What does Jackson mean by this statement?

2. Is Jackson's final statement a contradiction with the way he lived his life?

Record your answer in your history journal.

WRITING

Imagine that you are a teacher writing a report card for the United States between 1789 and 1850. Grade the nation in the following "subjects": *Democracy, Government, Geography, Foreign Relations,* and *Economics.* Briefly explain your reason for giving each grade. Conclude the report card by describing any areas of improvement that the U.S. should focus on during the next "term."

NAME _____

LIBRARY / MEDIA CENTER RESEARCH LOG

DUE DATE _____

Brainstorm: Other Sources and Places to Look

Places I **Know** to Look

What I Need to **Find**

I need to use:

☐ primary
☐ secondary

I need to use: ☐ _____ primary _____ sources.
secondary

WHAT I FOUND

Title/Author/Location (call # or URL)

How I Found it

	Suggestion	Library Catalog	Browsing	Internet Search	Web link

Primary Source	Secondary Source

Rate each source from 1 (low) to 4 (high) in the categories below

helpful   relevant

Book/Periodical	Website	Other

LIBRARY/ MEDIA CENTER RESEARCH LOG

NAME _____

DUE DATE _____

What I Need to **Find**

[box]

I need to use:

- [ ] primary
- [ ] secondary

sources.

Places I **Know** to Look

[box]

Brainstorm: Other Sources and Places to Look

[box]

WHAT I FOUND

Title/Author/Location (call # or URL)

	Book/Periodical	Website	Other	Primary Source	Secondary Source	Suggestion	Library Catalog	Browsing	Internet Search	Web link	helpful	relevant
	☐	☐	☐	☐	☐	☐	☐	☐	☐	☐		
	☐	☐	☐	☐	☐	☐	☐	☐	☐	☐		
	☐	☐	☐	☐	☐	☐	☐	☐	☐	☐		
	☐	☐	☐	☐	☐	☐	☐	☐	☐	☐		
	☐	☐	☐	☐	☐	☐	☐	☐	☐	☐		
	☐	☐	☐	☐	☐	☐	☐	☐	☐	☐		

How I Found it

Rate each source from 1 (low) to 4 (high) in the categories below

LIBRARY/ MEDIA CENTER RESEARCH LOG

NAME _____

DUE DATE _____

What I Need to **Find**

I need to use:

☐ primary
☐ secondary

sources.

Places I **Know** to Look

Brainstorm: Other Sources and Places to Look

WHAT I FOUND

Title/Author/Location (call # or URL)

How I Found it

- ☐ Suggestion
- ☐ Library Catalog
- ☐ Browsing
- ☐ Internet Search
- ☐ Web link

- ☐ Primary Source
- ☐ Secondary Source

- ☐ Book/Periodical
- ☐ Website
- ☐ Other

Rate each source from 1 (low) to 4 (high) in the categories below

helpful   relevant

NAME _____

DUE DATE _____

Brainstorm: Other Sources and Places to Look

Places I **Know** to Look

What I Need to **Find**

I need to use:

☐ primary
☐ secondary

sources.

WHAT I FOUND

Title/Author/Location (call # or URL)

How I Found it

- Suggestion
- Library Catalog
- Browsing
- Internet Search
- Web link

- Primary Source
- Secondary Source

- Book/Periodical
- Website
- Other

Rate each source from 1 (low) to 4 (high) in the categories below

- helpful
- relevant

NAME

LIBRARY/ MEDIA CENTER RESEARCH LOG

DUE DATE

What I Need to **Find**

I need to use:
- ☐ primary
- ☐ secondary

sources.

Brainstorm: Other Sources and Places to Look

Places I **Know** to Look

WHAT I FOUND

Title/Author/Location (call # or URL)

How I Found it
- Suggestion
- Library Catalog
- Browsing
- Internet Search
- Web link

- Primary Source
- Secondary Source

- Book/Periodical
- Website
- Other

Rate each source from 1 (low) to 4 (high) in the categories below

- helpful
- relevant

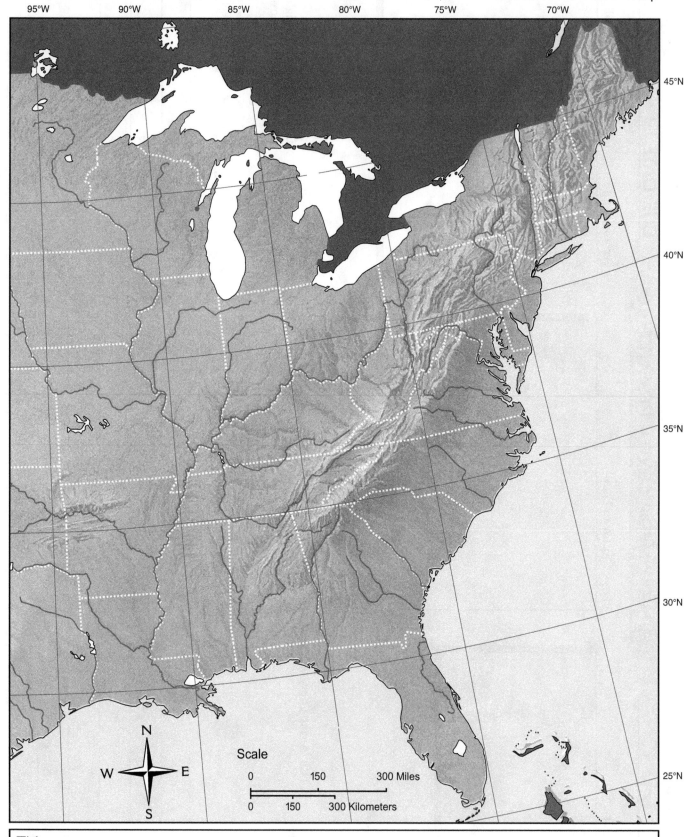

95°W 90°W 85°W 80°W 75°W 70°W

45°N

40°N

35°N

30°N

25°N

N
W E
S

Scale

0   150   300 Miles

0   150   300 Kilometers

Title

Legend

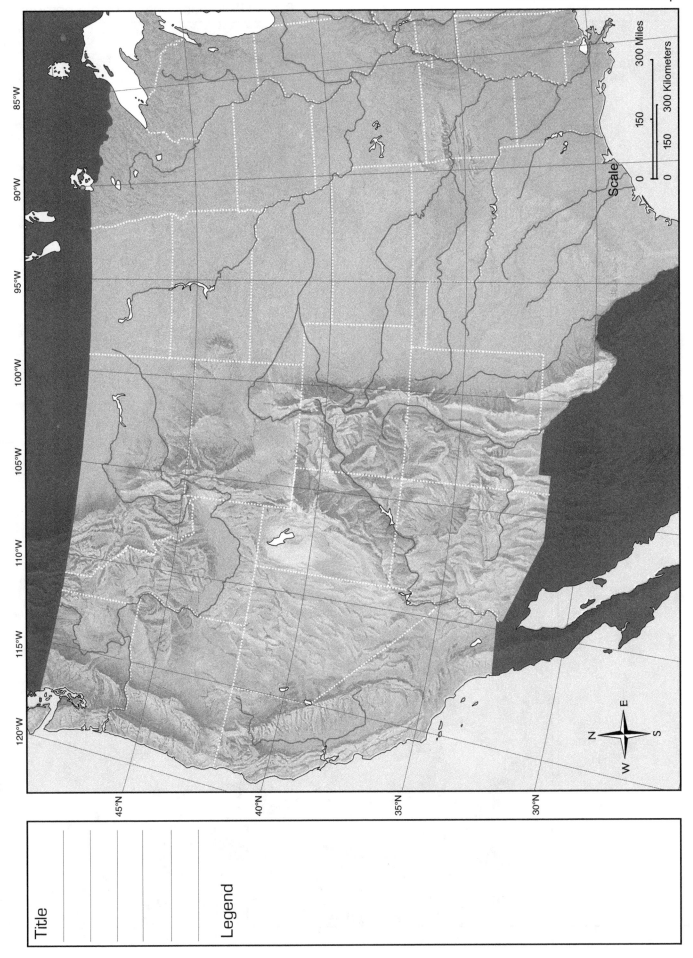

Title

Legend

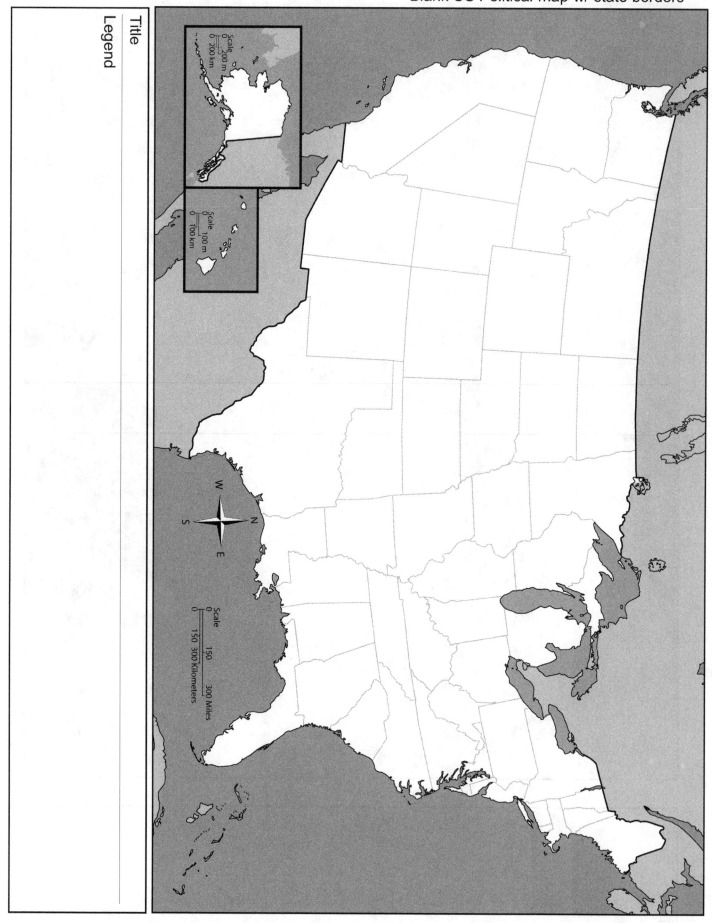

Title

Legend

Scale
0   200 km

Scale
0   100 km

Scale
0   150   300 Miles
0   150 300 Kilometers

W   N
S   E

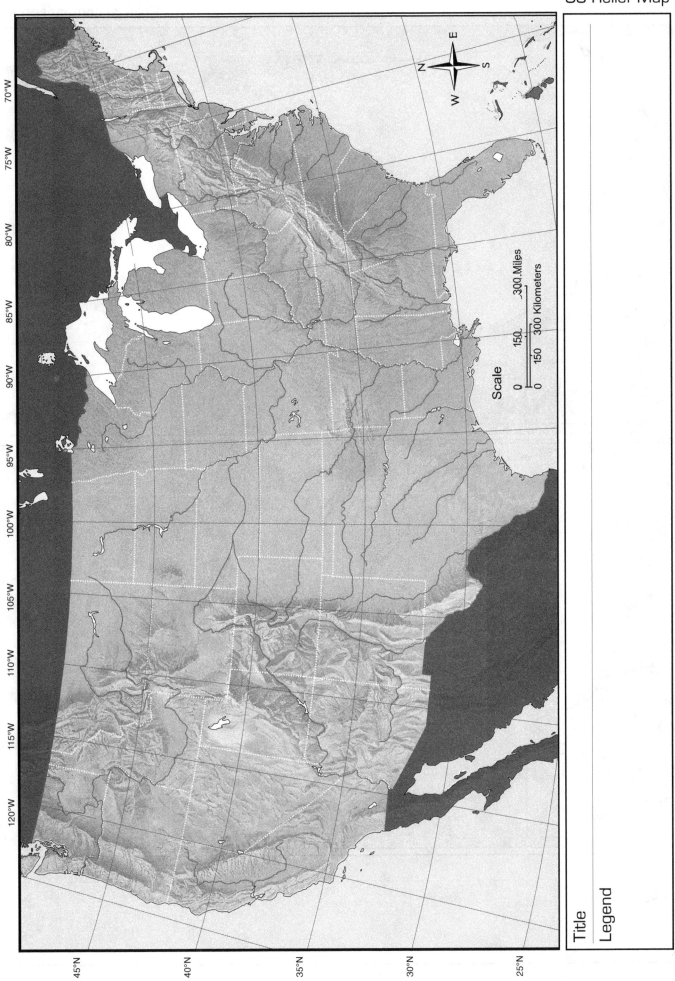

Scale

300 Miles

300 Kilometers

150

150

300

0

0

70°W
75°W
80°W
85°W
90°W
95°W
100°W
105°W
110°W
115°W
120°W

45°N
40°N
35°N
30°N
25°N

Title

Legend

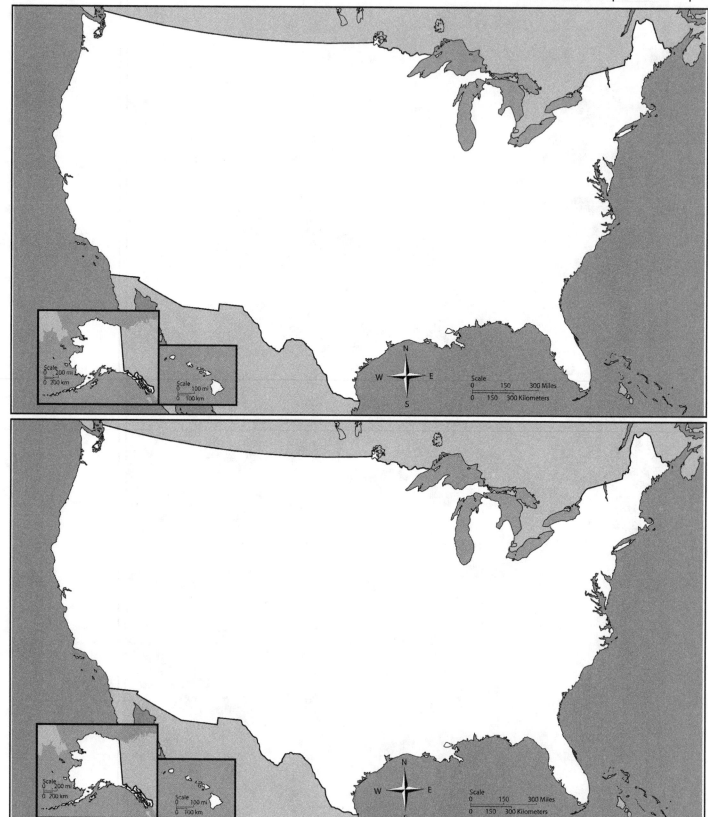

Scale
0   200 mi
0   200 km

Scale
0   100 mi
0   100 km

N
W   E
S

Scale
0   150   300 Miles
0   150   300 Kilometers

Scale
0   200 mi
0   200 km

Scale
0   100 mi
0   100 km

N
W   E
S

Scale
0   150   300 Miles
0   150   300 Kilometers

Title

Legend